START BEING WHO YOU WANT TO BECOME.

The ultimate guide on how to become your ideal self.

STANLEY RAPHAEL.

Table of Contents

Chapter 1:

Visualize who you wish to become:

You must first improve within before your life may improve outside. This calls for certain procedures. Your thoughts and feelings influence how you behave. We become what we think. Your life is shaped by your activities. You will ultimately start putting your intentions into action if you begin each day by imagining the life you desire as if it were already here, followed by positive affirmations, and precise intents to support your affirmations. Your good deeds will then produce good outcomes. Your life will change on the outside as you change within.

The brain is prepared for change by three practices. They consist of intentions, vision, and affirmations. Each day should begin with one of these three exercises. A positive outlook on the life you want, positive affirmations of that outlook, and positive intentions you commit to carrying out every day to make your vision a reality are the building blocks of positive change. It takes repetition to alter the brain. For the rest of your life, you will need to continuously work on your imagery, affirmations, and objectives. The brain does not delete either. The old, harmful neural networks go inactive when new ones are created, yet they persist.

To keep your visualizations, affirmations, and goals strong for the remainder of your life, you will need to continue using them every day. If not, they will fizzle out and you run the danger of reverting to your old, default way of being, perceiving, and acting. The same brain networks that would fire if our fantasies become reality are activated when we see ourselves truly living the life we want. We set our minds up to take action to fulfill our aspirations by envisioning them. According to others, visualizing opens up our creative unconscious. The creative process includes visualization. We finally convey what we perceive via behavior. The Universe responds to the positive energy we emit, as is true with the

Law of Attraction. It returns to us the good vibes that others have for us.

This is how visualizing makes us more likely to attract the things we want. We can do everything we can think of and believe in. To enhance their performance, elite athletes employ visualization. Similar to this, imagining our ideal lives helps us perform better while trying to make such lives a reality. Visualization supports the clear and intentional design of our life. Additionally, visualization inspires us to take action to realize our aspirations. It motivates us to exert the required initiative and effort to make it happen. There is more to visualization than merely imagining the results you seek. It's also about developing a better awareness of who you are, what drives you, what obstacles stand in your way, and how to come up with a concrete strategy with short- and long-term objectives that will enable you to surpass your expectations. When done correctly, visualization may be very effective in reaching any objective. using your mental imagination and seeing yourself already having achieved your objective. Imagine having everything you want and experiencing what it is like to have it. You can only perceive something in your "inner world" before you can do it in your "outside world."

Chapter 2:

find out your purpose and what you want in life:

What's my life's purpose? is a perennial question. Aristotle was considering the meaning of life and formulating his theory of teleology, or the notion that everything in life has a purpose, as early as the fourth century BC.

Finding one's life's purpose seems more crucial than ever in the modern, technologically advanced world when we are constantly being tugged in several ways. Many individuals spend their whole lives reacting to events rather than taking action and identifying the needs and beliefs that motivate them. They often confuse their mission with a short-term objective, even though they believe they are aware of it. Many other people who are asking themselves this question want to find meaning in life, but they are unsure of how to do it. We naturally only feel content when we are doing something to better ourselves or our lives. Every aspect of life is urging us to develop. We begin to experience pain, fear, and worry when we cease developing. As we turn around and observe what others have that we don't, we become vulnerable to jealousy.

We begin craving prestige, financial possessions, and power instead of questioning, "What is my purpose in life? But eventually, all of those things will leave you feeling empty. Setting goals, such as purchasing a home or starting a company, gives you a feeling of accomplishment and is crucial to leading the life you want. These objectives are elevated even more by purpose. Goal achievement does not guarantee pleasure. Therefore, once you ask yourself, "What is my purpose?" you're seeking development and a sincere sense of fulfillment. And finding happiness is a need, not a luxury or a pastime.

How to Find Your Life's Purpose.

Knowing your mission has a lot of advantages, but how can you do that? The path to pleasure and meaningful existence is created by combining the science of success with the art of fulfillment. You must learn to strike this equilibrium if you want to discover your mission.

1. LOOK INWARD:

The answers to the questions "What is my purpose in life?" and "How can I be happy?" are the same. By listening to other people's ideas and looking for outside acceptance, you will never fully comprehend how to establish your purpose. You already own all you need.

The only thing holding you back is your restrictive notions. With each limiting thought you identify and swap out for an empowering one, you become more self-aware. When you have control over your emotions, you can live your life as you like.

2. PRIORITIZE THE PURPOSE ABOVE GOALS.

You won't ever discover your actual passion or figure out how to find your purpose if all of your attention is on accomplishing short-term objectives. Your goals must always be based on figuring out your objective. If they're not, you'll only feel content for a little period before you start seeking elsewhere. When setting a goal, think about how it will increase your sense of fulfillment. How does this connect to my goal? To make sure that your mission is constantly in the forefront of your thoughts.

3. PAY ATTENTION TO WHAT YOU HAVE:

Having an abundant attitude is similar to opening your eyes to life; you will see goodness and beauty wherever you look. Your life's purpose becomes clearer with this new outlook.

You feel like you have more answers and are closer to reaching important objectives, so you start to wonder less and less about how to discover your purpose. Fear leaves us and abundance shows up when we concentrate on what we already have. You'll stop worrying that your life is a waste and start attracting pleasure and optimism. Finding your meaning changes from being a difficult objective to an exhilarating adventure.

4. TAKE RESPONSIBILITY FOR YOUR LIFE:

You can only find true satisfaction by creating your own life. You can achieve something remarkable by doing this. You must choose correctly and be aware of it in your heart and soul if you want to discover your destiny. You must not allow anxiety or fear to rule you.

It won't provide an answer to the query "What is my purpose?"When you find your goal on your own, rather than blaming others, you will feel fulfilled. The. A choice chosen out of fear is seldom the right one. It won't provide an answer to the query "What is my purpose?" but will just make things more complicated. You must give up playing the victim if you want to take responsibility. Recognize that your choices, not those of others, are the cause of every condition in your life. When you find your goal on your own, rather than blaming others, you will feel fulfilled.

5. CONSIDER WHAT MAKES YOU HAPPY:

Consider your life's history and note the moments that brought you the greatest happiness. Was it during the time you two were interacting? delivering an effective presentation at work? Making an art or giving back? You often find your interests when you learn what makes you happy. Examine your skills as well since they are related to that feeling of joy: Can you create a realistic portrait with a pencil? Do those who know you well say that you have a good ear? You'll probably discover hobbies that you may develop into a successful job when you pay careful attention to the activities or abilities that come easily to you and also make you happy.

6. CREATE A PERSONAL LIFE VISION STATEMENT:

To answer the question "What is my purpose?" you must first understand the ideal world and your place in it. Finding out what life would be like if everyone was achieving their full potential is a necessary step in developing a life vision statement. This will assist you in creating a road map that will lead you on the right way.

7. IDENTIFY YOUR REAL NEEDS:

Some individuals aren't even sure where to begin when they question themselves, "What is my mission in life?" If this describes you, it might be helpful to look at the Six Human Needs. Every choice you make is influenced by your primary desire, which may be a contribution, love/connection, diversity, love/significance, or assurance. Lack of self-awareness might cause you to have a false feeling of purpose that is dependent on other people's expectations. This explains why you may have the greatest physical health of your life, climb the job ladder to the top, meet the "ideal" mate, and yet not be happy. Your deepest wants come first in seeking fulfillment.

8. FORMALIZE YOUR STORY:

Writing aids in the organization of our ideas as well as the discovery of fresh ones. It has been shown to aid in goal achievement, memory enhancement, and stress reduction—all of which are crucial while learning how to discover your purpose. Writing about your life might uncover hidden meanings that you would not otherwise notice. Begin with this activity: What qualities do you possess that have enabled you to overcome challenges? How do you assist others? And how have others been able to assist you? When you put everything in writing, patterns will start to emerge that will aid in identifying your purpose.

9. GIVE YOURSELF TIME:

Answering the profound question "What is my purpose?" requires thought and contemplation. You never have time to simply sit quietly and re-establish contact with yourself when you're always rushing from one engagement to another. Make sure to block off enough time for yourself so that you can tune out the outside world's demands and noise and concentrate on what you desire. Take a deep breath and find your center if you're feeling worn out by your quest for purpose in life. Spend some time for yourself, whether it means visiting a spa or relaxing with a book in the park. Your values—the convictions you hold most dear as a compass for your life—can be found by searching inside. Without initially taking a step back and unwinding, you won't know how to discover your mission.

10. ACKNOWLEDGE ACCEPTANCE.

Recognizing your limits is a necessary step in discovering your mission. Give yourself a break rather than becoming upset with yourself. Learn more about oneself gradually by acting as an observer. You may discover the significance you're looking for when you develop self-compassion and self-awareness. Being tolerant of oneself entails practicing self-compassion. It may be incredibly unsettling to feel lost in life. Even though you may be irritated, be kind to yourself. Every person who has ever asked themselves the question "What is my purpose?" started in a state of ambiguity.

Because of their hesitation, they dug deep and discovered deeper significance.

11. LOCATE YOUR COMMUNITY:

Finding where you fit in is often the first step in determining your life's purpose. We feel at home, at ease, and free to be who we are when we are around our "people." Your community can often assist you in learning how to locate your mission or after you've discovered it, how to live it. Follow your interests to discover your community. Engage in voluntary work. Enroll in a class to learn a skill you like. Look for the assistance online. Find others who share your taste in plays, literature, or music. You are who your friends are, and when you discover the perfect community, it can only be a wonderful thing.

12. BE VERSATILE:

Letting go of previous identities and activities that no longer serve us is one of the most difficult aspects of learning how to discover your purpose. However, it still has to be done. As you develop and evolve, your life's purpose is likely to do the same. You must be prepared to be adaptable and to pay attention to your deepest needs and desires. Finding your mission requires a lifetime of effort. You may grow your integrity while maintaining loyalty to who you are by being adaptive. What is my mission in life? will be a lot simpler to answer if you define your basic beliefs and stop looking for outside validation.

Chapter 3:

Put up a strategy to accomplish your desire:

Nothing is more powerful than realizing you have accomplished your goals. Sometimes we let our self-limiting thoughts and justifications keep us from aiming as high as our hearts want in our ambitions and objectives. There are many excuses we might give ourselves for why we won't ever succeed in achieving our goals.

We may believe we lack the resources—time, money, strength, or support. Maybe we think we're not good enough, clever enough, or skilled enough to achieve our goals. Perhaps it's because we're stressed out or think achieving our goals would be unattainable. We will repeatedly demonstrate that we are wrong in life if we go through it thinking we cannot accomplish our objectives. We not only risk losing our enthusiasm and feeling of optimism, but we also run the risk of ceasing to dream completely. We all deserve prosperity and pleasure, it's true. Our purpose in life is to experience all that it has to offer.

We have the chance to gain important life lessons that encourage us to believe that everything is possible when we continue along the path of following our aspirations. We might easily lose focus when we consider all of the processes and unknowns necessary to realize our ideal. The loftier the goal, the more overwhelming it may seem. This sense of "overwhelm" might often stop us from even taking the first step.

Here are 7 tried-and-true methods for making your aspirations and objectives a reality.

Approach #1.

Enjoy establishing your objectives: When you get there, picture the feelings you wish to have: As if it were already a reality, enter that sensation. You can know where you are going with the aid of the effective technique of visualization. Knowing our destination makes it simpler to follow our gut feelings and remain on a course that is in line with our reality.

Don't forget to make your aspirations and objectives big and to produce visual representations of them. Keep those recollections nearby. When you reach your stopping point and need to be reminded of "why" you began out and "why" you don't want to quit, you will need them.

Method #2.

Put your attention on making little progress toward a goal: Give yourself permission to just take one step at a time rather than stressing about how many there will be.

Approach #3.

Write out your objectives: Make a monthly plan for the things you want to concentrate on first. Then, develop a weekly and daily summary of the tasks you'll be working on; be sure your plan is doable. You end up spending less time overthinking and worrying about all of the numerous tasks and projects you have to complete once you transfer all of the details from your mind onto paper (or a computer). Downloading your game plan should take a little time each month. Then you can utilize that time to accomplish things rather than waste a lot of time worrying.

Approach #4.

Ensure that you set aside some time every day to "laser concentrate" on doing one minor activity that is part of your weekly or monthly game plan: The Key is consistency. We might get disoriented and lose track of where to begin when we spend too much time considering the larger picture. Just keep your head up and concentrate on one little thing at a time. Dream generation is a process, not a sprint.

Approach #5.

With the key individuals in your life, share your dreams to generate excitement for whatever it is you are doing: It is much simpler to keep your dreams concealed and never bring them to light when you keep them a secret. People who are behind us and are aware of our lofty goals serve as our support system. They are the people we turn to when the road becomes depressing and we need trustworthy individuals to reaffirm "why" we first began.

Method #6.

It's natural for the path to our goals to be rocky; it's not supposed to be smooth and too simple: All of our valuable learning and possibilities are found in the bumps. We can doubt ourselves often, and we might also feel helpless and defeated. To battle all that is difficult and painful, we could even be inclined to strain ourselves to exhaustion. We typically know we need to take some time for ourselves when the road gets overwhelming.

Make a firm commitment to yourself not to lose delight in the trip by becoming too concentrated. Taking care of yourself regularly is essential to realizing your ambitions. You won't fall behind if you take frequent pauses to refocus and refuel. You may employ your newly found energy and enthusiasm after recharging your batteries. We always have the option to restart, which is much preferable to giving up or losing confidence in the dream itself.

Approach #7.

completing each interim objective along the road, don't forget: This enthusiasm and thankfulness will give you the drive and self-assurance you need to feel like you can accomplish your BIG ambition. Remind yourself often that realizing your ambitions is a journey rather than a sprint. Celebrate and take pleasure in your trip as much as you can, but most importantly, treat yourself well while it. You'll thank yourself for it afterward.

You develop yourself while you work toward achieving your objectives. When you see what you are capable of, you continue to dream up aspirations that will guarantee a complete, joyous, and rewarding life path. There is never a better moment than the present to start living your goals, so gather your vision board, dream list, dream declaration statement, and anything else that helps you achieve your goals.

Admire your goals and express gratitude for how they motivate you to develop into the person you are today. All you need to do is be clear about what you want and take actionable measures to get there. There will be some obstacles in your path, but if you use the appropriate methods and tactics, you'll have a greater chance of achieving your goals.

Chapter 4:

Be dedicated, committed, and passionate about achieving your desire:

Success necessitates making certain promises. We must acknowledge that not everything will go our way. It is simple to give in to irritation and entertain notions of failure when we encounter difficulty or any kind of delay on our journey. When we are struggling, we are unable to understand our feelings. We are unable to envision how things will change for the better and we are incapable of making the greatest judgments.

Even though you may not have any influence over the current situation, if you stick to your goals for success, you will ultimately succeed. You shouldn't give up on your goal just because the route you're traveling was previously obvious but is now unclear. Decide to maintain focus on the task at hand. Dare to do things a little bit differently, even if it means defying the status quo if the way things have always been done is no longer working. Do what has to be done, but do it morally and without disparaging or infringing upon the rights of others. You are you. Stay faithful to your principles, beliefs, and work ethic while adding your special touch. Keep moving ahead in the manner that only you can since you are a unique experience that cannot be duplicated. Nothing inflames us more viciously than the frustration of working toward our goal in vain. Commit to recovering your course if you are feeling unsure. Reconnect with your inner self and the drive behind your initial concept.

Your agenda is reset when you reconnect with the "why" of what you're doing. Additionally, it gives you the inspiration you need to keep going. You may alter your sails more as you sketch out your course. Writing things down makes them clearer, so never undervalue the impact of this simple yet useful action. The things you write down are considerably more likely to get accomplished than the ones you don't.

Your final destination is not uncertain. Setting new long-term objectives is a part of resetting your schedule. Commit to set objectives that will increase your success level. In addition to giving you a clear path to follow, goals also provide you with a tool to track your development. You get insight into what shorter-term objectives must be accomplished to pave the way for those longer-term objectives by working toward your longer-term goals. The golden pot at the end of the rainbow represents your long-term objectives. You need to have these goals in front of you to stay motivated and on track. Longer-term objectives give you hope and motivate you to take action. Your life grows happier the closer you get to them. Suffering allows you to develop, learn, and advance.

Embrace the idea that things may improve through changing. You must be unyielding, focused, and dedicated to advancing your profession, changing your course, and achieving where you want to go with newfound motivation and optimism throughout uncertain times.

Uncertain times should not be used as an excuse to slow down and give up. It's a good idea to check your direction sometimes. This is something you should do often since it stimulates original ideas. You are less likely to stray from your course when you can respond to queries of this kind. Asking questions may help you gain perspective, elevate your head, and transform ambiguity into clarity. What do you see as a more successful individual handling uncertain and hopeless circumstances in their career? Take hold of your vision and put it into practice in your own life. Decide to be calm. Develop the maturity you need to take care of yourself. Rushing and avoiding both reflect impulsivity, reactivity, and fear. Step by step and just concentrate on striking the ball in front of you as you go ahead. Moving on to the next phase should be done carefully and with a feeling of accomplishment for the previous step. By proceeding in this manner, stages are not missed and you learn where you must stand up for your rights and triumph over adversity. To achieve anything worthwhile, you must be willing to repeatedly pick yourself up off the ground.

Give yourself permission to look after, nurture, and prioritize yourself, particularly if you've been working in the background for a long time. Pull back and take a nap if you're feeling worn out by the world around you. All legendary fighters need rest. Rest implies recharging, not stopping or giving up. You will reflect from the outside world how much respect and enthusiasm you have for yourself as an individual. There isn't a shortcut to success. Don't use shortcuts, lies, cheating, or theft to advance your career. Commit to achieving success in a sincere, moral, and patient manner. The rewards you get will increase as you perform more, particularly in terms of reputation. The truth, like the cream in the coffee, will ultimately rise to the surface and reveal all the shortcuts, drama, rumors, and underlying dishonesty that allowed cheaters, liars, or drama-creators to succeed. Although they may ascend swiftly, these people will collapse violently.

Don't assess yourself against others. You are you. You will succeed if you believe in what you do, if you commit to your success, and if you have unshakeable conviction in your cause. Decide that you won't let a poor moment in your life affect your mental condition in the future. Naturally, the road to success is much longer than a day, but over the length of a lifetime, the challenges are only a brief moment in time as you pursue your goals. Success fluctuates, just like everything else in life. Don't allow a brief experience with hardship cause you to become negative in your outlook moving ahead. The purpose of downtime is to improve your fundamental level of training. Make it a point to improve rather than stay angry. Success cannot be desired while you wait for it to come to you.

You must go outside and take it. Whether you're just beginning your career, striving to meet the requirements to join Club, or on the executive track and want to advance, commit to becoming noticed. Right now, what has to happen for you to advance to the next level is your hard work, the quality of that job, and the way you treat others. There are three options available to you if you are unhappy with your current situation. You may either keep doing what you dislike, try to modify how you see what you are doing and find methods to like it, or take a risk and entirely alter your course. By selecting option 3, you decide to take a chance on the known to create the unknown. We need to continually commit to taking risks. Without significant risk, there can be no true success. Be prepared, adaptable, and most of all, willing.

Chapter 5:

Resist the fear of failure:

Have you ever avoided doing anything because you were so frightened of failing? Or maybe you unconsciously sabotage your efforts to prevent the potential of a bigger failure because you were afraid of failing? This is undoubtedly something that many of us have gone through at some point.

The dread of failure may paralyze us; it can keep us from acting, which prevents us from advancing. But when we let fear stand in the way of moving ahead in life, we stand to lose out on a lot of wonderful chances. What Gives People a Failure Fear? We must first define what "failure" genuinely means before we can identify the root reasons for this dread. We all define failure differently simply because we all have different standards, ideals, and worldviews. For someone else, a failure can just be a terrific learning opportunity. Push through your fear of failing and continue to work for your objectives. Many of us, at least sometimes, are terrified of failure. However, fear of failure occurs when we let this fear prevent us from doing the acts that might help us advance toward realizing our objectives. Numerous factors might contribute to the fear of failure. For some individuals, having critical or unsupportive parents is a contributing factor.

They carry the bad sentiments from their childhood into adulthood since they were often undercut or made to feel inferior. A distressing experience that happened to you might also be a contributing factor. Say, for instance, that a few years ago you delivered a crucial presentation in front of a large audience and performed horribly. It's possible that the experience was so awful that you developed a fear of failing in later endeavors. And even now, years later, you still have that anxiety. It's almost impossible to live a full life without failing in some way. People who do this are presumably living such careful lives that they stay put. Simply put, they aren't alive.

But the great thing is that we get to choose how we interpret it. Failure might be seen as "the end of the world" or as evidence of how inadequate we are. Alternatively, we might see failure as the fantastic learning opportunity that it often is. We have the option to search for the lesson we are supposed to learn after every failure. These lessons are crucial because they help us learn and prevent repeating the same mistakes. Failures can only stop us if we let them.

Consider the chances you'll lose if you let your failures discourage you. Failure may also help us discover something about ourselves that we otherwise never would have known. For instance, failure might show you how resilient you are as a person. You might find your closest friends or unanticipated inspiration to achieve through failing at something. Often, the best ideas are the ones that follow a failure. Success in life depends on accepting and using such revelations. It's important to understand that failure is always a possibility in anything we do. In addition to being brave, taking that opportunity and running with it provides us with a richer, more fulfilling existence. Many of us sometimes experience fear of failure, but we must not allow that fear to keep us from taking action.

There are many reasons why we fear failing, ranging from things that happened to us as children to errors we've made as adults. It's critical to understand that we are always free to choose whether or not to feel fear. Establish objectives that will boost your confidence. Learn to think positively, have backup plans, and objectively weigh all probable outcomes. we can decide whether or not to feel fear. Establish objectives that will boost your confidence. Develop contingency plans, practice thinking optimistically, and learn how to objectively investigate and assess all potential scenarios. You'll start to conquer your fear by pushing ahead gradually and gently. You'll start to conquer your fear if you go ahead gradually but steadily.

You claim to be aware of your poor self-esteem and negative thought patterns. Being aware of these things is beneficial because it allows you to choose what you want to do about them. I understand that hearing advice to think more positively may be challenging, but positive thinking is a very potent tool for boosting self-esteem and counteracting self-sabotage.

Chapter 6:

Don't go the extra mile to please people or give attention to how they feel about you:

Being polite or pleasant to other people is not intrinsically immoral. In actuality, it's a fairly useful quality. But sometimes we act in this way to keep from disappointing other people or to put pressure on ourselves to live up to a certain standard. People-pleasers often make a deliberate decision to behave in this manner out of fear of offending others.

Although it is a fantastic method to avoid confrontation, doing so will wear you out and make you miserable in the long term. Being true to yourself is challenging if your actions and words are constantly being influenced by what you believe other people desire. It becomes simple to spend the bulk of your energy trying to make other people happy rather than trying to make yourself happy. Because of this, engaging in this activity ultimately results in low self-esteem, a sense that there are too many demands of you, and the failure to build effective coping mechanisms. The most crucial thing to keep in mind while acting is to be genuine to yourself.

Avoid acting in a way that will make you seem attractive to others, and instead, stick to what you know is best for you. Don't be scared to maintain your ground if you've been forced to do something you don't feel comfortable with. It demonstrates your independence by demonstrating your strength. You may quit trying to satisfy everyone, but not by becoming someone you are not. People will appreciate you more if you stay true to yourself. Sometimes it's necessary to remind yourself that it's OK to say "no" since people-pleasing may become such a deeply entrenched habit. When someone asks you to do something you don't want to do, or if they make an unreasonable or impossible request, it's OK to put your needs first and say "no." Additionally, you need to quit agreeing to tasks just because someone else asks you to do so if you aren't benefiting from them in any way. The most crucial element of this is to constantly remind yourself that taking care of yourself doesn't mean being selfish; it means saying "no" when you mean it. People-pleasers often lack awareness of the limits they must establish in their own life.

But you may begin by being aware of your actions. It may seem challenging at first, but you must begin to pay attention to what is occurring and recognize what needs to change. Make a list of the things you now do, such as bringing coffee for a colleague, that make you feel sad or used, and rank them in order of significance, placing the most important items at the top. You won't feel the need to compromise who you are by using this straightforward technique. Setting boundaries enables you to refuse requests from those who are abusing your time or asking for assistance. Keep in mind that you are not being selfish; rather, you just have enough self-assurance in who you are to realize that it is OK not to always comply with demands. Life is a trip, and along the way, you will come across a lot of individuals who will have requests for you. To win someone over, you can find yourself acting as their doormat. The issue with this is that it will prevent you from being pleased and from exercising your judgment. It is unhealthy to live to please others and may result in emotions of tiredness, tension, and even sadness. It's critical to take charge of your life and understand how significant you are. It might be hard to change a habit of pleasing once it has taken hold.

But everything is achievable given enough time, patience, and persistence. So keep in mind that you deserve happiness too when you're feeling stressed or worn out because of the folks for whom you've been doing your best. You're not merely attending to the needs of others. Don't overlook the needs you have for yourself.

Chapter 7:

Learn from the mistakes, falls, and failures you encounter on your way.

Some errors may seem to be the end of the world from the outside, but they provide you the chance to grow, learn, and become a better version of yourself.
Consider all of life's errors you've made and how they have shaped your character and abilities.

Think about all the skills you've learned through your failures, as well as how they've affected your knowledge, personality, social growth, and life experience. Errors have value. However, before you can appreciate them, you must first recognize them as an important and valuable aspect of your life that you cannot escape and must instead welcome with an open mind and heart. Who knows, if you're willing to learn from the experience and develop from it, your worst failures can wind up being your most dazzling successes.

The Risks of Fixating on Errors.

When errors are committed, there is often a desire to linger on, regret, or despise them. Many individuals react to errors in this way out of instinct, but you shouldn't react to mistakes in this way. Your self-confidence and ability to express yourself creatively will suffer if you dwell on errors. Your performance and productivity will suffer, and you'll feel awful all the time. Additionally, dwelling on errors may lead to perfectionism and procrastination behaviors, as well as a wide range of negative emotions including anger, stress, anxiety, fear, and frustration. There is no way to live like this. You can see how many individuals are completely misinformed when you realize that errors may be a beneficial and transformational force in your life. This tendency to concentrate negatively on errors generally dates back to your early years, when you were either mistakenly taught to avoid making them or, if you did, your parents or guardians saw them as undesirable and undesirable aspects of life. Although your experience may have been different, likely, making errors wasn't seen as a necessary and advantageous part of growing up.

Benefiting from Mistakes:

It's possible that as a youngster, you were taught to keep your faults to yourself so that other people couldn't point them out to you or make fun of you. This could help you feel a bit better initially. But deep down, the remorse you feel about your error will consume you. The psychologically best course of action is often to acknowledge your error and accept full responsibility for rectifying the situation after making a mistake. This will not only earn you the respect of your colleagues, but it will also leave you stress-free. Because of your error, you are now in charge of making things right and taking lessons from it for the future. This is the proper state of affairs. Although they sometimes refuse to acknowledge their errors, individuals rarely learn from their blunders. And as a consequence, unless important lessons are ultimately learned, people keep making the same errors over and over again.

Acknowledge and Forgive Your Mistakes
Being at peace with your errors entails that you are at ease with them and willing to accept whatever lessons you can from the situation. You must remember a few things, however, to get to this point in your life. First off, keep in mind that the route to your objectives will inevitably be littered with blunders, errors in judgment, unanticipated events, and poorly prepared actions. This is only a logical aspect of existence. We're not flawless; that much is true. Because nobody is flawless, faults will be made by everyone. They are what give life meaning and enjoyment. In actuality, the larger the errors you ultimately commit, the bigger the lessons you learn, and the more you develop as a

consequence, giving you a wider range of life experience and insight. However, it's crucial to keep in mind that you are not your errors. Errors are a result of your actions, not who you are. You must not conflate the two. Second, it's critical to acknowledge that mistakes are growth opportunities. Making mistakes is not a step back; rather, it is a side-step that, as you go forward, will enable you to view the route ahead with more clarity.

They are there to support you and keep you in check as you go toward your goals. Constant failure and errors lead to success. Nobody in this world has ever accomplished anything significant without experiencing significant failure and making an absurd number of errors along the way. It won't be any different on your travels. Be at peace with it and realize that making errors is just a part of life.

Change the way you think about errors.

Stop seeing errors as something unpleasant and damaging. Instead, start thinking of errors as chances to rethink the course you are pursuing to achieve your objectives. Is it possible that making a mistake can lead you to a shortcut you had previously missed? Or maybe, as you go along your trip, it will provide you the opportunity to master a crucial talent that will be essential for your future. In truth, failures provide the best chance to become stronger and more resilient. You can keep moving ahead despite the challenges and failures in your path if you have resilience. And the more errors you commit, the more robust you'll become, provided you actively learn from them and modify your strategy. Making mistakes gives you the chance to improve your behavior. Perhaps what you're doing won't be successful in the long run. Therefore, the error you made today may have made you aware of this issue. If you fix it, you'll be in a lot better position going forward. Making mistakes gives you the chance to review your choices. Sometimes, the choice you make may not be following the objectives you have in mind.

Making a mistake will show you that you are heading in the wrong direction. Use it to turn yourself around and get back on the correct track. They are good at two things when you make blunders. They should firstly show you that you are pushing yourself. Every time you put a challenge on yourself, you're developing and picking up new skills. Making mistakes also shows that you have the potential to grow. This is an encouraging development. What would be the purpose of accomplishing anything at all if there was no possibility for development or improvement? Life would be inert because we would already be where we wanted to go. We have something to aim towards when there is hope for progress since it gives us something to put out the effort for. You must learn to accept that making errors is just a natural part of learning; they serve as everyday opportunities for practice and training leading up to the achievement of our main goal.

You practice every day to accomplish that major objective, much as a boxer would in preparation for a big match. And just like a boxer, you will be struck and knocked out. You could fall flat on your face after slipping repeatedly. Yes, you messed up, but you also got back up and carried on. Your focus is on the larger picture and not on the immediate error you committed. Accept the error and use it as a learning opportunity, but don't allow it to deter you from your ultimate goal. While Making Mistakes, Exercise Caution. It's critical to avoid the temptation of attempting to defend your error when you make a mistake. Errors must be accepted rather than excused or explained. You won't ever genuinely learn the lessons you need to master to advance in this area of your life until you accept responsibility for your errors. Ignoring whatever errors you make is equally risky.

Your errors serve as guideposts that properly point you. You run the danger of drifting off course if you ignore these directional cues. And the more work it will ultimately take to get yourself back on the correct course in the future, the longer it will take you to recognize this. Making errors doesn't feel pleasant at first. You were undoubtedly taught as a child that making mistakes was terrible, but as an adult, you shouldn't ever wallow in self-pity or regret. In the long run, this type of conduct is never beneficial and merely stunts your development. It's important to avoid placing blame—including blame on yourself—when you make a mistake.

Simply accept responsibility for it, take action to address it, draw lessons from it, and move on. Realize that if you start blaming yourself or finding reasons why you made a mistake, you are wasting your time. For the majority of individuals, being defensive-minded is natural, but it cannot be natural for you. Stop whining or offering justifications. Instead, get feedback on the error and record your observations to help you learn from the situation and make better judgments and actions moving forward. Making errors indicates that you are balancing success and failure.

However, those who have experienced the most failures are often the ones who are ultimately rewarded with the greatest achievements. These individuals braved failure and dared to fail rapidly by making as many errors as they could to learn from their failures and modify their actions appropriately. After all, the player with the best chance of ultimately succeeding is the one who picks up the game's rules the fastest. After it comes to being focused and motivated when errors are made, optimism is an imperative need. But in addition to optimism, you also need the courage to face uncertainty, curiosity to ask the right questions that will lead to the solutions you seek, persistence and determination to work through any problems that may have arisen as a result of your error, and humor to help you get through those trying times when everything seems lost and you can't seem to find the solutions to your problems. You'll have to rely on yourself.

This does not exclude you from seeking support or assistance from others. It does, nevertheless, imply that you are resourceful enough to get whatever you need to deal with your errors in the most advantageous way feasible.

Chapter 8:

Apply the power of imagination: be it until you make it.

Who do you wish to develop into? What degree of success are you aiming for? Which personality do you wish to have? What kind of image do you want to project? Every child has a hero they want to be like as they grow up. It doesn't matter whether it's our parents, grandparents, teachers, coaches, or anybody else. Everyone has found inspiration in someone who pushes them to improve themselves.

 In our line of business, we all know that one person who has achieved the level of success we would want to achieve or someone who leads such a wonderful, fulfilling life that other people may only dream of. What kind of hero do you want to resemble, and how do you achieve that? These are questions you could ask yourself.

It's quite straightforward; in fact, you won't believe it. We have to start behaving like the person we want to be to become that person. "When ONE is ready for a thing, it puts in its APPEARANCE," a group of psychologists corrected. Your mind and the world begin to function in intriguing ways once you begin behaving like the person you want to be. Simply said, your mind begins to alter as you start thinking, behaving, and believing like that individual. Then, as soon as you begin to behave in this manner, you begin to develop this behavior. Regardless of what you believe, nice things begin to come your way from the universe or God. It can tell that you're prepared to fill that role.

But the actual inquiry is: Are you ready to become the person you've always imagined yourself to be? Will you devote your time and energy to being that person? Will you put in the necessary effort and do what it takes rather than merely dreaming it? I'm sure you have this idealized image of yourself in your head when you think about your future and what it would feel like to be living your dream. This individual speaks differently, dresses differently, and carries themselves with confidence. They also behave differently. They behave and make choices in a manner that is distinct from your own. Most individuals are unaware that to start achieving their objectives, they must first take steps to truly become this person.

I refer to this individual as your true self or true You. You should always consider what your true self would do when faced with a dilemma. Being the person you want requires you to be honest with yourself and consider how you should behave. By making these choices, you are naturally moving toward your objectives since you are putting in the effort and beginning to act in ways that will advance you. Therefore, if you make the proper decisions every day, your results will come sooner than you anticipate.

Chapter 9:

Act with the mindset of a winner:

Being a winner requires more than just behaving or even thinking like you. To be properly regarded as one, you must have the necessary traits rather than merely having the appropriate appearance. If you haven't already realized it, the mentality is the one thing that separates winners from failures. Long enough and you'll start to see the effects of thinking and acting like a winner. Eventually, you'll know how to approach anything like a winner by following your instincts.

Confidence is one of the keys to winning. You may see yourself winning if you have confidence. You can then genuinely succeed. I'm ready to bet you that nine out of ten of the individuals in your life who you are envious of how they got where they are would answer that they either believed in themselves or worked hard for it.

Since you have to believe in yourself to get it done and work hard for anything, these two answers are simply variations on the same theme. You can move mountains if you have confidence. Moving mountains will also inevitably boost your confidence.

This is a self-sustaining cycle that only requires a little amount of your work. Don't you desire a higher sense of self-worth? Then you must begin to believe in yourself because, if you do not, no one else will. But once you do, you'll start achieving things that you would not have thought possible for you. Your well-earned pride in those achievements will motivate you to carry out even greater and more impressive feats. See how the cycle functions? It may swiftly transform a loss into a very successful winner.

The attitude of a victor

We've been discussing this all along, but if there's one thing I've seen in the past that prevents losers from turning into winners, it's that they don't comprehend this. Understanding the attitude of a winner is crucial since it is impossible to succeed without it. You must consciously decide that you want to change before putting in the effort to do so.

You can't have it done by anybody else. So, if there is one thing you learn from this, it should be that your mind is something you can alter if you want to advance in your quest to succeed. The attitude of a winner is centered on confidence, but there are other crucial components. For instance, maintaining composure and tranquility is crucial. Someone who seems to be successful and often screams at others is not a winner; instead, they are a jackass, most likely a very unhappy jackass. Anger, avarice, and pessimism are further bad characteristics. Nobody likes to be furious, yet losers often are, while winners seek out peaceful resolutions. To some level, greed is a wonderful thing, but excessive greed will make someone insane and unhappy forever. And last, victors don't dwell on the drawbacks. Instead, they strive to alter them since, with the proper perspective, every issue can be resolved.

How do you cultivate a winning mentality?

You must concentrate on what you desire if you want to cultivate a winning mentality. Winners pursue their goals to succeed. Winners go out and grab things, while losers have to wait for them to be given to them. If you want to succeed, you'll pursue what you want, and success will come effortlessly to you. Everyone aspires to be a winner because winners unquestionably enjoy their life more than losers. But it will take some effort and some contemplation to achieve it. You can resolve your issues if you are prepared to examine yourself and adjust the things that are not functioning. Being a winner demands the proper attitude and cognitive process, which might be challenging and seem odd at first but eventually becomes your identity. If that seems like too much effort to you, then being a winner is not for you. For the rest of you, however, I strongly suggest giving it a go since success is worth it.

Chapter 10:

Don't give up, only you can stop you:

If you're fighting not to give up, you've probably faced your fair share of obstacles, hardships, and rejection. You may be sick of hearing that "whatever kills you makes you stronger" and that it teaches you how to maintain your optimism and persevere in your pursuit of success. You should feel pleased with yourself for continuing to try. Following that, you may focus on creating a mentality and work ethic that will ensure success if you keep pursuing your goals. Take on a more upbeat outlook.

Even though it could be difficult for you to remain optimistic when you feel like you've tried everything and nothing is working for you, it's crucial to do so if you want to never give up. Being upbeat helps you recognize all the great aspects of your life that you would otherwise miss out on if you were to concentrate just on the drawbacks. [1] Additionally, since you'll be approaching life with a "can do" mentality, you'll be more receptive to chances and possibilities. It is real. Being more upbeat will not only help you overcome obstacles, but it will also enable you to accept new ones. You won't be able to advance if you're resentful or fixated on all of your failures.

Try answering your negative statement with two positive ones if you notice yourself gripping or moaning. Although you shouldn't feel like you're faking it when you seem happy but are depressed, you should be aware that the more you pretend to be happy, the more gradually you'll start to see the good side of life. Having a positive attitude may be improved by being around individuals who are joyful and help you enjoy life more. It will be challenging to have a positive outlook and feel like you shouldn't quit if all of your pals are negative and depressing. You must be able to roll with the punches and not just accept change but revel in it if you want to work on cultivating the correct mentality for perseverance. You may have been shocked when your lover unexpectedly dumped you or when your family revealed that you would be relocating to a new location, but you must learn to adjust to a new situation, concentrate on the positive elements of it, and develop a strategy for prospering in it. Consider change as a chance to broaden your horizons, learn something new, and interact with new people.

Even if you may not yet be able to perceive any advantages to the circumstance, you should be pleased with how you handled it and how you continued. Take note of your errors. You must adopt a mentality that enables you to accept the errors you've made and learn from them to avoid encountering the same issues in the future if you want to be able to persevere. When you first make a mistake, you may just feel disheartened or ashamed, but you should take a step back to analyze what went wrong and develop a strategy for avoiding the same error in the future. Nobody likes to make a mistake, but errors teach you how to see potential issues before they arise. For instance, you could think that dating a possessive lover who broke your heart was a big mistake, yet this misstep early in life may save you from choosing the wrong partner later. Don't pretend that you couldn't have done anything differently. You won't ever learn if all of your attention is on appearing flawless.

Recognize that there will always be more chances to succeed. You must believe that there will always be new opportunities for success if you want to concentrate on never giving up. Though living in the moment is crucial, you should strive to be thrilled about the future rather than believing that it holds nothing for you. If you have the mindset that you somehow missed the boat, fantastic possibilities will never present themselves since you won't be able to notice them. You could think that since you didn't get the ideal job for which you went through three rounds of interviews, you'll never find a profession that fits you, but in the long run, you'll discover that there are many jobs out there that feel just right for you, even if it takes some time to find them. Additionally, you might concentrate on expanding your idea of success.

Get educated: You must keep accumulating information and learning more about life and the position you're in if you want to develop a resilient attitude that will help you thrive and not give up. There is always more for you to learn and more possibilities to pursue if you have a passion for knowledge and are enthusiastic about the world. Whether you're attempting to market your book, get a new job, or apply to college, you can learn more about whatever it is you're trying to accomplish. The more you know, the better equipped you'll be to manage any challenges that come your way. The best method to learn is, of course, to read as much as you can. This might be reading books, the news, or online research on your topic of interest. But you may also learn by conversing with authorities in your industry, making an effort to network, or seeking out guidance from knowledgeable individuals.

You won't be able to fully give up as long as you remain conscious of the fact that there is still more for you to discover. If you persevere, wonderful things will occur. You could be considering quitting because you want success to come to you immediately, which is another possible explanation. You could believe that things should have worked out for you simply because you submitted ten job applications, sent your book manuscript to five agencies, or went on four dates with various men. However, failure is a common part of the journey to success, so you shouldn't give up before you even begin to attempt. Talking to others who are going through the same thing might sometimes be helpful. To wrap it up, pursuing the life you desire, you need to be committed and diligent. The pursuit of a dream is tied to answering your life's biggest question. That query arises from inside your inner man and it is your mission to find the answer. If you go away from this world unfulfilled without discovering the answer, you will have denied yourself the opportunity to live your dream life.